thank you Jesus
for being my saviour

written & illustrated by Darcy Jackson

Published by Fictitious Ink Publishing, Tumbler Ridge, BC, Canada, V0C 2W0

This booklet is
devoted to Lord Jesus
and dedicated to
my grandchildren;
Ryder and Finley.
I hope the messages
bring you joy and courage.
I U
Nana

John 15: 9 - 11

As the Father has loved Me, so have I loved you. Now remain in My love. If you obey My commands, you will remain in My love,... I have told you this so that My joy may be in you, and that your joy may be complete.

Thankyou Jesus for my Joy!

2 Corinthians 3:17
Now the Lord is the Spirit, and where the Spirit of the Lord is, there is freedom.

John 8:36
So if the Son sets you free, you will be free indeed!

Thankyou Jesus for my freedom

5

2 Corinthians 3:18
We are being transformed into His likeness with ever-increasing glory which comes from the Lord, who is the Spirit.

2 Corinthians 10:5
And we take captive every thought to make it obedient to Christ.

Romans 12:2
Do not conform any longer to the pattern of this world, but be transformed by the renewing of your mind.

Ephesians 3:20
Now to Him who is able to do immeasurably more than all we ask or imagine, according to His power that is at work within us, to Him be glory in the church and in Christ Jesus throughout all generations, for ever and ever! Amen.

9

Psalm 69:14
Rescue me from the mire, do not let me
sink. Deliver me from those who hate me,
from the deep waters.

Psalm 18:28
You, O Lord, keep my lamp burning; my
God turns my darkness into light.

2 Timothy 1:6,7
I remind you to fan into flame the gift of
God which is in you,... For God did not give
us a Spirit of timidity but of power, of love
and of a sound mind.

13

John 6:63
"The words I have spoken to you are Spirit and they are Life!"

Hebrews 4:12
For the Word of God is living and active. Sharper than any double-edged sword, it penetrates even to dividing soul and spirit, joints and marrow. It judges the thoughts and attitudes of the heart.

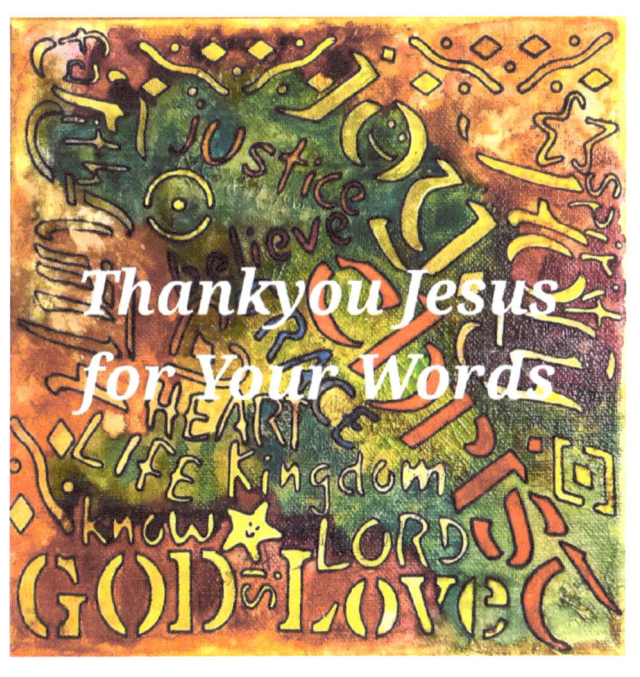

Thankyou Jesus for Your Words

John 11: 25, 26

Jesus said to her, "I AM the Resurrection and the Life. Whoever believes in Me will live, even though he dies. And whoever lives and believes in Me will never die. Do you believe this?"

"Yes Lord", she told Him. "I believe that You are the Christ, the Son of God, who was to come into the world!"

17

Joshua 1:7
Be strong and very courageous!

1 Timothy 6: 12
Fight the good fight of faith! Take hold of
the eternal Life to which you were called
when you made your good confession.

Matthew 16: 15, 16
Jesus asked, "Who do you say I AM?"
Peter answered, "You are the Christ, the
Son of the living God."

19

Colossians 1: 15, 16, 17
He is the image of the invisible God, the
Firstborn over all creation. For by Him all
things were created: visible and invisible;
whether thrones or powers, or rulers or
authorities. All things were created by Him
and for Him. He is before all things, and in
Him all things hold together.

Thankyou Jesus,......
for everything!

Psalm 23: 5
You prepare a table before me in the presence of my enemies. You anoint my head with oil; my cup overflows.

Matthew 5: 34
Then the King will say to those on His right, 'Come, you who are blessed by my Father; take your inheritance, the Kingdom prepared for you since the creation of the world'.

Thankyou Jesus for Your provision

Romans 5: 2 - 5
We rejoice in the hope of the glory of God.
We also rejoice in our sufferings because
we know that suffering produces
perseverance; perseverance, character;
and character, hope. And hope does not
disappoint us, because God has poured
out His Love into our hearts by the Holy
Spirit, whom He has given us.

Hebrews 6: 19
We have this hope as an anchor for the
soul, firm and secure.

Thankyou Jesus for giving me hope

25

Romans 5: 6 - 9

You see, at just the right time, when we were still powerless, Christ died for the ungodly. Very rarely will anyone die for a righteous man, though for a good man someone might possibly dare to die. But God demonstrates His own love for us in this: while we were still sinners, Christ died for us. Since we have now been justified by His Blood, how much more shall we be saved from God's wrath through Him!

27

Hebrews 4: 15, 16

For we do not have a High Priest who is unable to sympathize with our weaknesses, but we have One who has been tempted in every way, just as we are, yet was without sin. Let us then approach the Throne of Grace with confidence so that we may receive mercy and find grace to help us in our time of need.

Psalm 34: 18
The Lord is close to the broken-hearted and saves those who are crushed in spirit.

Ezekiel 36: 26
I will give you a new, undivided heart and put a new spirit in you. I will remove from you your heart of stone and give you a heart of flesh.

31

Ephesians 5: 8
For you were once darkness, but now you
are Light in the Lord. Live as children of
Light (for the fruit of the Light consists in
all goodness, righteousness and truth).
Find out what pleases the Lord.

1 Peter 2: 9
You are a chosen people, a royal priest-
hood, a holy nation, a people belonging to
God; that you may declare the praises of
Him who called you out of darkness into
His wonderful Light.

33

John 8: 12
Jesus said, "I AM the Light of the world. Whoever follows Me will never walk in darkness, but will have the Light of Life".

2 Corinthians 4: 6
For God who said, "Let Light shine out of darkness", made His Light shine in our hearts to give us the Light of knowledge of the glory of God in the face of Christ.

Thankyou Jesus for being the Light of my life

Romans 1: 3, 4
Regarding God's Son,... who through the
Spirit of holiness was declared with power
to be the Son of God by His Resurrection
from the dead: Jesus Christ our Lord.

Romans 8: 11
And if the Spirit of Him who raised Jesus
from the dead is living in you, He who
raised Christ from the dead will also give
life to your mortal bodies through His
Spirit, who lives in you.

RESURRECTION POWER

Thankyou Jesus for raising
new life from the dead

37

1 John 4: 16 - 19
God is love. Whoever lives in love lives in
God, and God in him. Love is made
complete among us so that we will have
confidence on the day of judgment,
because in this world we are like Him.
There is no fear in love. But perfect love
drives out fear, because fear has to do with
punishment,... We love because He first
loved us.

Thankyou Jesus for loving me. Amen

39

1 Corinthians 13: 4 - 8
Love is patient. Love is kind. It does not
envy, it does not boast, it is not proud. It is
not rude, it is not self-seeking. It is not
easily angered, it keeps no record of
wrongs. Love does not delight in evil but
rejoices with the truth. It always protects,
always trusts, always hopes, always
perseveres. Love never fails.

41

Lord God, I pray that you would forgive me of my sins. Come into my life, Lord. Make me a new creation. Come into my heart and my mind and cleanse me from all unright-eousness. I want to be born again. Lord, lead me in Your ways. Guide me in truth in all my ways, for all my days, and let them be Your ways. Lord, my life is in you.

Amen.

More in the series!

We hope you found this inspirational
pocketbook uplifting. The simple
affirmative statements, illustrations,
and scriptures were prayerfully compiled
by the author to bring you
strength and peace.

Plus, there are more books in the series!
They'd make a beautiful gift for someone
you love. Available at select bookstores
and online. God bless!

*If you enjoyed this book, please consider
leaving a positive rating or review.*

www.ingramcontent.com/pod-product-compliance
Lightning Source LLC
Chambersburg PA
CBHW040905120626
46551CB00006B/653